County Council

Libraries, books and more.........

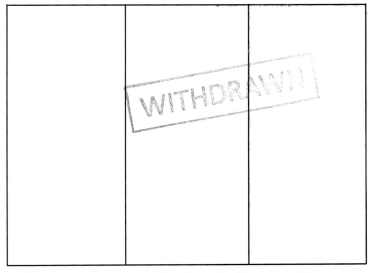

Please return/renew this item by the last date due.
Library items may also be renewed by phone on
030 33 33 1234 (24 hours) or via our website

www.cumbria.gov.uk/libraries

Cumbria Libraries

CLIC

Interactive Catalogue

Ask for a CLIC pass

INDEPENDENT INNOVATIVE INTERNATIONAL

Published by Cinnamon Press
Meirion House
Tanygrisiau
Blaenau Ffestiniog
Gwynedd, LL41 3SU
www.cinnamonpress.com
The right of Caroline Davies to be identified as author of this work has been asserted by her in accordance with the Copyright, Designs and Patent Act, 1988. Copyright © 2016 Caroline Davies.
ISBN: 978-1-910836-24-8
British Library Cataloguing in Publication Data. A CIP record for this book can be obtained from the British Library.

Designed and typeset in Palatino by Cinnamon Press. Printed in Poland.
Cover design by Adam Craig from original artwork by Caroline Davies.
Cinnamon Press is represented in the UK by Inpress Ltd www.inpressbooks.co.uk and in Wales by the Welsh Books Council www.cllc.org.uk

Contents

For Victor and Percy
and all the men who did not return from the war
and for Jeremy Banning and Vanessa Gebbie
who took me to the battlefields.

Voices from Stone
and Bronze

The Litany

She has to look down as the roll call begins.
She knows all of them, each name, every family.

Thomas Arnold, G Arthur Caffrey, Thomas Cudworth,
                                        T Owen Davies
and then the moment of her son's name when she raises her head.

It does not help, knowing he was surrounded by friends.
His officer wrote he died bravely and cheerfully.

She does not believe a word of it.
Other families have had similar letters.

It does not help. She wants him back
even if he were mutilated or in a wheelchair.

Or like Gwilym who scarcely knows the day or month.
It is not her place to hold Gwilym's hand,

as his sister does to keep him quiet.
There is nothing to be done for any of them.

Going over

Here I am just a cog in the army that grinds towards the horizon.

Here I am with a letter to my parents, unable to think of what to
say,
    writing 'I'm only doing my bit',
    I lean against the sandbags, draw on a cigarette,
    watch the sunset turn the sky orange and pink,
    feel my body shudder with the roar of the bombardment,
    shiver before dawn, my feet on the ladder.

Here I am, lit up by Verey lights and star shells.
Here I fall to the ground.
Here.

Skin I

After Jane and Louise Wilson — Undead Sun

In the end there was nothing you could do but take off your uniform, tear the arms from the jacket, rip the trousers apart piece by piece, then your underpants and vest, until you were stripped, until everything hung in shreds from the barbed wire.

Thiepval Memorial: The Lost Men France (2014) by Paul Emmanuel. Courtesy of the artist and Art South Africa.

Skin II

After Paul Emmanuel — Lost Men

In the autumn of 2014 if you walk away from the Thiepval Memorial with its lists of the missing, go behind the trees and across a ploughed field you will find what remains of Paul Emmanuel's work; his banners, with the indelible print of his body, strung from crosses and exposed to the elements all year. You will be the only one to visit on this soft grey afternoon and as you stand beneath the long pale strips, fragments will fall onto the ground.

11

The Sculptor and The Fusilier:

Sergeant Cox goes to the studio

The sculptor, Mr Toft, has a complete uniform
for me to put on.
I tell him the last time I wore khaki
my skin was crawling with lice.
He says vermin might make it more authentic,
but it would be difficult for me to keep still.
He shows me his sketches of soldiers.
'Thing is', I tell him, 'it wasn't like that.'
He says he knows they are not fully realised.

That's why he wanted me.
I get changed behind a screen.
The uniform stiff and new, buckles to be yanked into place.
I have to be methodical, it steadies your nerves before an attack
to have everything orderly.
If I was going to meet my maker,
at least I'd started the day tidy.

They said it was an honour to be chosen
but I would get paid for it.
Standing in his studio. I hope he's remembered.

He's staring at my rifle.
I've shouldered arms, an automatic gesture.
'Shouldn't that have something on the end?'
He means for me to fix my bayonet.

Always the last thing you did.
That rasp repeating along the line of men.
When I do as he tells me, he flinches at the sound.
Or perhaps it's the sight of an arm's length of steel.

Towards the end we broke into the Hindenburg Reserve line.
Myself and another lad captured a machine gun
with the necessary butchery.

12

Nobody else was left
after that gun had done its work.
The only time I used my bayonet.

I ask him how long he reckons
they will leave the statue up.
He says bronze lasts a long time.
Stands up well to British weather.
He seems surprised at my question.

He asks if I've heard of Michael Someone.
I haven't. He fetches a book
to show me what he calls a masterpiece.
A bloke with no clothes on,
but with a well muscled chest, strong neck.
He'd be useful in a scrap, I'd say,
provided he was properly dressed.

I tell Mr Toft I'm glad I'm keeping my clothes on.
He says he made a memorial for the Boer war.
The men who modelled for that one were less irreverent.
I've not been compared to a vicar before
I take note to watch my language
so as not to shock him.

It's being back in uniform does it.
I feel I should be ordering people about
including him, though he'd have been an officer
most like, he wouldn't have lasted five minutes
without someone like me to set him right.

Mr Toft prepares to go to work

He is exactly what I want.
A strong man with none of the scars,
tremors or blemishes of the others.
Still carries himself like a soldier.
Though he hasn't been in uniform
                    since the war was over.

I have my housekeeper serve us tea.
His hands huge against his china cup
as I try to put him at his ease. He scowls.
I take note of his broad shoulders,
arms accustomed to manual labour.
I wonder what he has been doing.

He has intense blue eyes
though for my purposes their colour does not matter.
A quick glance at his feet —
scuffed boots with worn down heels.
I decide against observing his legs
as he clearly doesn't like me looking.

I explain the purpose of the sitting
to enable me to draw, then mould
his form in clay. I show him the drawings.
He frowns and says they don't look like soldiers.
I instruct him to get changed.

Through the gap at the base of the screen I see his bare feet,
looking surprisingly cared for in appearance.
He comes out with the clothes he has shed
neatly folded in a pile on his arm.
He asks brusquely where he should stow them
so I indicate the Lloyd loom chair.

This is how it begins.
I don't want more words to pass between us.
But his rifle looks unfinished
so I have to ask.
He flourishes his bayonet
with some unnecessary violence.

I want to take in every aspect of him
before I ask him to move
as he would on the battlefield.
His left hand keeps going up
to scratch his neck as if he can't help himself.
I had the uniform adjusted by my tailor
to this sergeant's exact measurements
so it will be a perfect fit.
Perhaps he's nervous. He seems on edge.

I wish my assistant did not have influenza
and had got this man poised and ready.
I can hear myself babbling. I explain
I want my statues perfectly proportioned
so people can imagine them coming to life.
I show him Michelangelo's David.
He stands at my shoulder, a good head taller.
Close enough for me to notice
that intense smell of a man who doesn't bathe.

He contemplates the David in silence
then mutters about keeping his clothes on.
Such a familiar beloved figure
it had not occurred to me
my fusilier might find the nudity shocking.

Mr Toft waits

I tell him 'I won't talk while I draw
and I need you to be silent,
but as we discussed
I want you to move
as you would on a battlefield'

He stops scratching his neck.
A raised red welt below his cropped hairline.
He goes into a series of practised moves
with his rifle, up onto his shoulder
then down—parade ground stuff.

His eyes never leave my face
seeking a sign of approval.
I wait.

Sergeant Cox

Sergeant Cox thinks of his lucky rabbit's foot

I show him the usual stuff
like you'd do to impress an officer.
I can tell by his face,
this isn't what Mr Toft wants.

So I start doing my last minute checks:
Run my finger along the edge of the blade
to test its sharpness. Pat down my pockets.
I used to carry a rabbit's foot.

My mum gave it to me when I joined up.
It survived the Somme and even that final month
of 1918 when we went for the Hindenburg line.
I don't have it with me today. Didn't think
how it might come in handy.

Flesh Wound

I press the sculptor's forefinger to the bayonet
to show him how blunt this is.
How suddenly his blood wells up.

He snatches his hand back, sucks the cut.
His fingers must be softer than mine.
I can't feel how sharp it is.

I stammer apologies for doing him harm.
He holds his finger up.
'A flesh wound,' he says softly.

Sergeant Cox with Bayonet

Sergeant Cox uses his bayonet

Their machine gun has killed most of my men.
Two of us dash towards it,
as if we can outrun bullets.

We get close enough to hurl ourselves
into the gun emplacement. How I wish
for a Mills bomb to fling.

My rifle clenched in one hand.
The other fist raised
as if to ward off harm.

'Hold still,' the sculptor's voice, a single shot.
'That's perfect.' He circles me,
his pencil scratches across the paper.

I keep my eyes front.
He's warned me not to speak.
I scarcely dare breathe.

I thought I was going to die
when I threw myself over the rim
of that enemy parapet.

Landed on my feet.
In that moment of shock
I made good use of my bayonet on their gunner.

Got his blood all over me.
I can never forget his brown eyes
un-seeing in death.

I sweat in this new uniform.
The weight of the rifle drags on my arm
but I keep it level. The pencil scratches on.

The Tommy statue at Flers

My brother in bronze protects the City of London
and I, his identical twin, keep watch in France
in the village square where I guard the High street.
        He stands ready
        for when the call comes.
        We are cast from the same mould.
But I would drop my rifle
and desert my post
rather than fight again.

We killed a man, my twin and I.
He'd slaughtered most of our company
before we leapt on him.
        My twin stabbed him in the chest
        and guttural words and blood bubbled
        from his mouth.

Did he beg us for another chance?
        My twin said we must be quick
        Nothing to be done
        but finish him off.

Flers

Glad of my men

My brothers have forgotten me.
I was sent north to Oldham, a long way from the war.
I have men to command and I have to be resolute,
not like that milksop in France.

There were plenty of arguments
about where my troop should be placed.
We are too near the pub and I have no means
of dealing with the drunks
except by steely example.
I could run my bayonet through someone.
It doesn't take much to tip me into anger.

The years have not been kind.
My right arm aches with arthritis
but people raised funds for treatment
and we have all been cleaned.

I am glad of my men, the Manchesters,
so I will never be alone.

Out in France:

What Louis Doffman knows

That his father is foreign.
That being sent to the front
is a strange kind of homecoming.

That he loves being with the rest of the lads
who have him figured out as one of them,
have shortened his surname to Monty.

That he chose Mountford
for its English ring.
That he has lied in his letters home.

That he is afraid. That he can sense his blood
and it thuds in his ears
as the artillery booms.

That he has no faith in the advancing barrage
going ahead across open ground
to destroy the enemy.

That he does not know how he will kill
when he gets into the German lines.
That he hopes they will all surrender.

That his company must advance towards the sunken lane,
they've nicknamed Gloucester Road.
That there are lots of enemy machine guns.

That as he climbs out of the trench
with the rest of the lads
he feels lifted up as if by angels.

Pigeon Ravine

In memory of the 228 men, including Louis Doffman (who served as Lewis Mountford) of the Second Battalion, Worcestershire Regiment, killed in Pigeon Ravine, 29th September 1918

Their orders are to advance from the Limerick Trench
at five thirty am. Ahead of them the ground stretches
level to the horizon.

Their objective is the Hindenburg line.
No one has told them their attack is a diversion.

No cover but there is a sunken lane—Gloucester Road
a refuge from enfilade fire when they get there.

The outcome not known until ten am
when a survivor crawls back
through thickening mist to Limerick Trench.

No one had reached the sunken road.

After being issued with SS456 Burial of Soldiers

Private J McCauley, 2nd Border Regiment

I am attached to a company of 150 men.
We work in pairs.
Our task is to search for dead bodies and to bury them.
Two issues of raw rum are served to us daily.

Our most important duty is to find the identity discs,
from bodies, often submerged in water, in shell-holes
and mine-craters, like huge masses of white slimy chalk.

The job has to be done: the disc has to be found.
The work makes me squirm.
No matter how many times I put my hands
inside the soft white flesh and grope
in search of the disc, it still makes me shudder.

I've had to pull bodies to pieces
to find the necessary
so they will not be buried as unknown.
The remains of a fine brave man on a shovel.
Just a heap of maggoty stuff and bones.
This is what war means.

In the Burial Party

McCauley insists we follow the rules.
I tell him these fellas are well beyond saving.
Sod the regulations. But he makes me do it.
They have been dead for weeks
and when you're done with poking about
for the disc – you stink to high heaven.
I've taken to rubbing my hands and face
with one issue of the rum but it's no use,
I can't get the stench out of my nose.
They say McCauley was one of the firing party
for a lad who kept running away.
I reckon he's never forgiven himself
for being privy to an execution
of one of our own.

Peter Barton's Lessons of History

For the tunnellers at La Boisselle and also the missing at Fromelles,
whose bodies were not found until 2007

A trench is not just a trench.
Each one was dug out spade by spade,
the work of men who were also soldiers.

A tunnel is not just a tunnel.
This one shows pick marks in the chalk
and a perfectly square shaft
made by men who were miners before the war.

This passage is not just a passage.
Here are sappers John Lane and Ezekiel Parkes
listed among the missing. They have no headstones,
but eighty feet below ground Peter knows where they lie.

A map is not just a map.
This German one has a cluster of crosses by the sally port
where they knew the attack would start.
Each cross is a dead Australian.

This history is not the whole truth.
Only the ground, the archaeology, the archives can reveal
these men in their trench, in their tunnel, on this map,
at the point where history abandoned them.

Charles Sargeant Jagger:

How to make a man—Part One

It is outside the scope of this book to give instruction
      in the anatomy of the human figure.
A sound knowledge of the bone framework
      and muscular system is essential.

We first of all select our subject.
The next step is to determine the most appropriate
      way of representing it.
The usual method is to sit patiently and wait
      for inspiration.
An infinite waste of time.

Pin a large sheet of paper on the studio wall.
Write at the top the subject chosen.
Write beneath any words or phrases the subject implies.
Many of them will be useless.

Others will suggest to the mind
      possible compositions.
Take a piece of stick charcoal and sketch very simply
      and in as few lines as possible.
You will by now have got something
      on which to make a start.
Our next duty is to know something of clay.

How to make a man — Part Two

Place a lump of clay on a modelling stand.
The knife will be most useful
                    at this stage.
Confine yourself to broad flat planes
                    and entirely ignore all detail.
You will presently have fashioned
                    a rough shape.

From this stage wire tools will be employed
                    for cutting away the surplus clay.

The most important quality is the silhouette.
I would exhort you to spare
            neither yourself nor your design
but to test every variation of shape.
Now turn your attention to the next stage.

How to make a man — Part Three

This model must be a perfectly finished miniature
in which every problem of composition
and treatment has been solved.

Apprentice

Before the war I was apprenticed as a metal engraver.
My Dad's choice instead of all that art stuff.
Has taken me years to shake off
that early training of paying meticulous attention.
A sculptor must deal
with big silhouettes, be blind to the intricate.

I thanked God for evening classes
so I could make Dad happy by earning my keep
but dusk brought escape.
I'd wanted to be a sculptor since I was eleven.

I remember walking with Dad round Whitby Bay.
There was a man sat on a boulder
turning a lump of clay.
As we watched it acquired paws,
long sleek flanks, an Egyptian headdress
and then it was a Sphinx.

Back home I set to
with a block of sandstone
and a penknife trying to recreate what we'd seen.
Dad insisted I go and cut the Yew hedges.
'That'll teach tha to make things into shape.'

Clay

The war changed everything.
The shock of realising
of all the men I'd trained with,
my close comrades,
I am the only survivor.

The war changed everything.
That fierce fallow time when clay
was the stuff of mud on the bottom of the trench
mixed with men's blood
and God knows what else.

Lieutenant Jagger remembers his Corporal

In the dark I'd climbed down from our trench
to look for dirt to fill sandbags,
and then I was hit in my right shoulder.

My corporal crawled towards me,
through sudden bursts of heat, splinters of stone
as the Turks tried to finish me off.
I did not dare move,
half dizzy with pain,
my pocket ripped away by a grenade.

He steadied me through that moment of weakness,
his firm fingers applying a bandage
and then that slow drag all the way back to our lines.

It was only afterwards, lying in hospital,
that I realised he'd held his body
between mine and the enemy,
the whole time.

They shipped me to Malta, then home.
I never saw him again and he did not survive the war.
So I try to put a measure of his courage
into each of my statues, in remembrance.

Recovery

They tell me I've made a good recovery
but I have my doubts.

I dream of being buried alive
after the undertaker has screwed down the lid.

I lie still in my bed in the dark and quiet.
Wonder how long before my air runs out.

In the Making

It is what you do with your hands
that matters. I still have mine.
It was always my shoulders
where I was wounded. They told me
if that last bullet
had been a few inches lower
it would have hit my heart
and I'd have gone out,
snuffed between finger and thumb,
like a candle.

Mr Jagger asks his tutor Mrs Lillian Wade to model for him

'Humanity' at the Hoylake and West Kirby memorial

This will be really difficult,
I've asked Lillian to model for me.
She knows the form.
I want to represent 'humanity'
as a female figure with a crown of thorns,
embodying the women we fought for.

I work as fast as I can.
I'm conscious of her hands,
the way she holds her arms,
the front of her dress pushed out
by the swell of her breasts.
I don't allow myself to think
of lifting that dress by the hem.

When I have finished the work
the figure I have made from her
with long robes and a cowl
is described by the critics
as resembling a nun.

Private Edwardes

'Soldier on Defence', at the Hoylake and West Kirby memorial

Sometimes at night I hear them singing
as I try to get some rest.
Always so cheerful as they sang their way to the front.
I cannot do enough to bring them back.

Private Edwardes, always in trouble
with our commanding officers
but such a magnificent scrapper.
My statue scarcely does him justice.

Great Western Railway memorial—March 1921

The Committee does not like either of my designs.
One was to be a soldier carrying a crucifix,
the other was armed with a trench catapult
to remind people of how David
killed Goliath despite his small size.

I'm going to spend the morning
walking round Paddington station.
I might offer them the figure of a man
in uniform waiting for a troop train.
It was a common enough sight.

Last night I dreamt I was back on Malta
in hospital and in pain.
When the nurse brought the package of letters
from home, I cried, though I tried to hide my tears.
The first letters I'd had in weeks
arriving like a small miracle.

Paddington Memorial

Great Western War Memorial—December 1921

MacColl has written on my behalf
to the chairman of the Committee, Lord Churchill.
I am sick to the back teeth of their vacillations.
They've even asked for a change
from a figure to a bas-relief.
I've told them, 'The first scheme submitted
is the best solution. Anything further
would not be as good.'

MacColl at least likes my sketches
and has told the Committee
they 'stir those mingled feelings
of fondness, sorrow and pride
that a war memorial should evoke'.
I just want to get on with the work.

Planning the Royal Artillery memorial

I shall portray them as I remember them.
Their toughness the reason we won the war.

I want their memorial to last as long as the pyramids.

Evelyn, his wife, worries about Jagger

He cries out at night, and mutters as he thrashes about.
I've learned not to wake him
for he will fail to recognise me.
I am not a woman but some soldier.
'Give them rapid fire,' he shouts, 'kill the bastards.'
He burns with sweat and the sheets are quite drenched.

During the day he is my own sweet Charlie again
in his favourite yellow shirt
and always working. His skilful hands are so strong.
In the light the only fierce thing about him
is Bill, our Macaw who climbs on his shoulders
to see off all comers.

When the work has gone well he will sleep calmly
and I will lie awake and listen to him breathing.

After the Unveiling of the Royal Artillery Memorial

Sometimes we used to envy the dead,
even the unburied bits in No Man's Land.
For them the struggle, to shove aside
their fears, finally over.

Often I startle awake at night,
my heart too loud for the silence.
I've nothing left to dredge up.

The Euston Road Mob:

Euston Memorial — 'Albert'

Albert, Royal Navy

There are four of us.

I'm Albert and I spent the war at sea. There's Percy who was in the infantry and my pal Frederick of the Royal Artillery, and George. He wears the Royal Flying Corps uniform. George has cobwebs covering his face, or so Percy says. We don't know how he died. I wish they'd come to clean him up, but that won't happen until wreath-laying time. I expect he went fast, plummeted from the sky.

Mine was a gunshot wound in the thigh. Too high for the ship's surgeon to take off my leg. He kept feeding me rum. A cloth over his nose to blot out the smell, as the wound went rotten. I can remember his face as if he was still next to me.

These aren't our real names, the foundry man said he had to call us something not just; sailor, airman, infantryman, artilleryman. Apart from Fred I've not seen any of them since 1921 when we were lined up for inspection.

Mr Ambrose Neale made us, based on the plans of an architect chap named Mr Reginald Wynn Owen. From one side Wynn Owen looked normal, on the other an empty eye socket. Disfigured they used to call it. He was well pleased with how we'd turned out, correct in every detail.

There was a team of navvies, all muscle and ripple, a considerable amount of rope and pulleys to raise us onto our stations. It was only after they removed my harness I found I could only see Fred.

The Portland stone at our backs like a tomb and the idea is we're in mourning for those who didn't return, three thousand, seven hundred and nineteen men of the London and North Western Railway company.

We could hear Percy moaning about being back on sodding sentry duty but I don't suppose he ever stood guard with his head bowed, weapon reversed.

I've never seen so many crowds as on the day of the unveiling, women mostly. There was a man called Sykes, a plate-layer before the war. He'd got the Victoria Cross for going out from the trenches under fire, four times, to save the wounded. He was a small man, the wreath he laid at our feet was as high as his chest. The company chairman and Field

Marshal Haig spoke about loyalty, patriotism and the contribution of the railways.

Percy muttered throughout about those fatal promises that the wire had been cut and the Germans killed by the artillery barrage. We all know how Percy died. We've heard it that many times.

If only he'd been in a Battalion of eight-foot-tall bronze infantry, impervious to machine gunfire—why then they might have stood a chance.

Frederick, Royal Artillery

There's a man comes every Friday
to the patch of grass
that passes for a park.

I watch him from the corner of my eye.
He was in the army.
Don't ask me how I know.

No uniform now and his clothes
must smell. Sells that homeless newspaper.
Doesn't shift many.

Folks tell him to 'keep the change'
rather than take money from his hands.
He hasn't seen me on my plinth.

His eyes have the dulled look
of a man who finds himself
with the curse of having survived.

That shudder as you collect
bits of a fellow soldier for burial.
His hands hold a tremor like mine.

He looks at the lime trees, the straggly grass.
I strain towards him unmoving,
eight foot of bronze soldier he refuses to see.

Some afternoons he dozes on a bench,
sitting upright, eyes shut
but senses half alert in case of an attack.

I too was in the artillery
and I need to tell him not to feel guilty,
but he does not notice me.

I want to tell him not to be afraid
as it gets dark. He smells of drink
as he marches towards the night bus.
He still does not look.

Percy, Infantry

I died on the barbed wire.
You can't see that now.

The sculptor with his one good eye
has made me a man again.

Pulled whole from the furnace.
I am as I was

before that moment
of being impaled, my guts spilling out.

A German machine-gunner raised his sights
to blow my head off. An act of mercy.

Frederick

For me it was a bayonet,
a wrench in the chest
and hot as shell splinters.

Far below I saw this bedraggled doll
as the enemy wiped
his weapon clean of blood
on one of my legs.

An Unknown Airman, Royal Flying Corps

They are forever talking
That Percy fellow never ceases.
They call me George
but that's never been my name.

I don't know who I was.
I know I used to fly above the trench lines.
I don't want to remember
but Percy goes over and over his death.

I don't want to be flesh and blood again.
I just want peace.
I don't mind the buses or being
on a roundabout. At least
these days nobody notices us.

At first it was more than I could bear.
The women would come,
their hands laden with poppies
and the men in wheelchairs
would look at each of us
before they bowed their heads.

Percy, Infantry

I died on the barbed wire.
You can't see that now.

The sculptor with his one good eye
has made me a man again.

Percy's fears are loudest at night
when they've all gone home
and the streets are quiet.
If I could get my hands
on his mouth, his throat I'd shut him up.

Frederick speaks from the other side.
He has a fine voice; a baritone.
He sings and Percy falls silent
and we all pack up our troubles
as we go the long way to Tipperary.

Frederick still speaks to me occasionally.
The others have stopped asking,
'You all right George. Rest easy.'
Sometimes Frederick talks about books.
Dickens is his favourite.

A Tale of Two Cities. He said
he'd been to Paris for one leave
instead of going home.
Lots of girls but he preferred
looking at the pictures in the galleries.

Percy has no time for me. He thinks
I'm stuck up.
He wants to be on the other side
with Frederick and Albert.

Those two talk when they think
we're asleep. I wish Frederick
wouldn't worry.
I'm fine being hollow and bronze.

Albert too is glad to be free
of those bodily urges
that threatened to expose him.
It took him an age
before he confessed to Frederick.
Percy was snoring and I being mute
meant his secret would be safe. Frederick said
the important thing was he hadn't
acted on that impulse. Bad for morale.

Percy, Infantry

Pulled whole from the furnace.
I am as I was

before that moment
of being impaled, my guts spilling out.

An Unknown Airman, Royal Flying Corps

Time passed. They started to knock down
the old station. Took away the arch.
A man came to measure us up.
I'm eight foot, two inches,
quite impressive.

The man had nice hands, Albert said.
Percy was afraid
they planned to melt us down.
He sobbed all night like a small child.
I almost felt sorry for him.

Percy, Infantry

A German machine-gunner raised his sights
to blow my head off. An act of mercy.

Years later when Albert had seen
two men kissing on the street he told
Frederick about the ship's surgeon.
He didn't say the name but he
knew him in all his private places.

That was how Albert said it.

Frederick was quiet for a long time
before he asked 'And did you love him?'
'He held me in his arms as I was dying.'

Frederick

We're nearly a hundred years old.
The best part of being bronze
is that 'age does not weary us.'
I'm as fit as I was at thirty-two.
Albert looks neat, all ship-shape.

I saw my wife just once at the unveiling.
She had both our kids with her.
Never seen them again.
I still look out for them. Daft though that is.
My son no longer ten, my daughter older than seven.

Albert

I still catch glimpses of him,
any fair haired man in a clean white shirt
is enough to remind me.

Frederick

Not being able to move is the worst thing
We're stuck like those poor wounded blighters.
Trouble is I can imagine being in a shell hole
when you no longer have the strength
to keep your mouth and nose clear of the mud.

Percy

I died on the barbed wire.
You can't see that now.

The sculptor with his one good eye
has made me a man again.

Frederick

I'd give anything to be able to walk along the Euston road
all the way to St Pancras,
Do they still have the station café beside the trains?
I'd love a slab of fruit cake and a cuppa to wash it down.

Not being able to move doesn't bother the others.
Albert laughs 'I've got no heart, so nothing
to trouble me by beating faster.'

He does still notice other men.
He makes a sigh that has in it
something of a groan.

We don't have any manly parts.
Our maker left those out.

I think it would help Percy
if he could give himself
a bit of a rub. We all used to do it.

I'd pretend not to notice with my men.
It gave them rest,
a few moments of comfort.

Albert

Instead at night we hear Percy die.
He cries out as his belly is ripped open by bullets.
Trying to hold himself in.

                                        Percy

                    I died on the barbed wire.
                    You can't see that now.

                    Pulled whole from the furnace.
                    I am as I was.

50

Frederick

He's so young. He must have been underage.
Should never have enlisted.
If I could move, I'd give him my shoulder
for a pillow, was never able to do that for any of them.
Being soft was deemed bad for morale.

All I could do was sing.
It's all I can do now.

Percy

The sculptor with his one good eye
has made me a man again.

Pulled whole from the furnace.
I am as I was

Albert

That rumble coming from Tavistock Square
like a shell landing behind the lines.

An ominous quiet. Then people begging for help.
That's when George began to weep.

We could hear him above the sirens.
'til Percy told him to 'shut it'.

The seventh day of the seventh month.
I shall never forget it.

Frederick

If I couldn't talk to Albert I would go mad.
We all thought George was mute,
until he began to howl.

I told Percy to leave him alone.
'You all right George?'
I've lost count of the number of times
I've said that over the decades
without ever expecting a reply.
He managed to stop sobbing.

But I could hear his breathing,
a panicked sound, like he'd run a mile.
I was about to reassure him
when he made a noise.
His voice hoarse with lack of use.
My name said very slowly. 'Frederick.'

Albert's eyes gleamed with that sideways look.
'George?'

Not

My

Name.

'What are you called?'

An ambulance went past on the Euston road
with that wail echoing off the buildings
as it carried the wounded to the casualty clearing station.

We flinched, myself most of all.

                                                'Are we at war again?'
I could hear the shake in Percy's voice.

'That sounded like a shell' Albert joined in.
No sense in frightening the kid out of his wits.
'They won't expect us to fight again.'

But Percy starts to whimper
I don't know what to do. I can't sing,
not with civilians dying a street away.

Albert

They've closed all the stations
so there's crowds of people on the streets.
Everyone saying similar things
'Terrible—a bomb'
'Yes I'm OK. I'm walking home.'

Percy, Infantry

That moment
of being impaled, my guts spilling out.

Albert

I thought of those who won't ever go home.
I suppose that's why we're here.

An Unknown Airman, Royal Flying Corps

That bomb going off so close
Brought back scenes I've tried to forget.

Our poor bloody infantry.
Piles of corpses in No Man's Land.

Didn't know it was my voice
raised in a protest of keening,
until Percy tells me to shut up.

I'm scared the civilians might notice
how my chest wants to heave
and tears run down my face.
But they don't ever see
the memories we hold.

Frederick asks what my real name is.
I am called Noel.

Euston Memorial—'Noel'

I had a brother of Percy's age.

John.

It comes back in fragments.

Percy starts to make that choking sound.
Never happened before during daytime.

I wait for Frederick to take command
as he always does when he says
to Albert 'Christ, I don't know what to do.'

I know Percy like me can't shift,
I hear him try to free himself from the barbed wire.
I must remember how to do words.

Come. Here.
Listen. Percy
Stay safe with us.

My young brother John
liked to go to chapel
on Sundays with Mam.

If I'd been home instead of in France
I'd have made sure he didn't lie about his age.
When I got the news it was too late.

I flew above the lines.
I was not supposed to recover the dead.
But I knew his body was out there.
When I made a nuisance of myself
they sent me to another sector.

I'm more of a heathen than John was
but I can remember the words.
For Percy's sake I say them.

The Lord is my shepherd
I shall not want.
I sense Percy listening.

He maketh me to lie down in green pastures,
He leadeth me beside the still waters.
So unlike a battlefield.

He restoreth my soul.
Do any of us have souls?
I, at least, have my voice again.

He leadeth me in the paths
of righteousness for His name's sake.
It doesn't matter whether I believe.

I can't sing like Frederick but I can do my bit.

Yea though I walk through the valley
of the shadow of death.
They were told to walk on the first of July 1916
and to keep in orderly lines.

I will fear no evil for thou art with me;
I'm not confident I can remember the rest
so I say forever and ever amen.

We can still hear the wounded in the square
though their cries might be in our heads.
But Percy seems to be at peace.

Albert

Frederick is silent. I can't even hear
him breathing like I normally can.
Has this morning been too much?
There have been bombs before in London
but after they rang all the bells for peace
we didn't speak of it.

Frederick?

Nothing.

I think of the first time I held Martin.
One of the crew had died, after he lost his footing
and fell into the hold. There was nothing the surgeon could do.

He'd hidden away but I found him
trying to compose himself in private,
as he wept about the lad's death.

'You won't tell anyone will you?'
I never made the promise
because in that moment of wanting to give comfort
I felt his body react to mine
so I purged his grief.

Noel, Royal Flying Corps

I do not know if they ever recovered John
or if fragments of his body still lie
in some forgotten corner of a French field.

Mam would read to us in the evening
from the Child's Garden of Verses
as lovely to my ears as the New Testament.

I try only to remember his face
lit by the candle's steady flame,
his lips moving as he repeats the words.

Percy, Infantry

I never knew Noel was kind.
All these years I've stood
beside his silent disapproval.

Even his voice is gentle.
He says the trick is to watch for clouds -
to think that when it arrives,
the rain will wash us clean.

I'd never noticed how
it makes our faces and uniforms shine.

Noel likes to be alone with his thoughts,
especially in the mornings when there's crowds.
I try not to bother him.

I can ask what he's thinking and he will answer.
He loves the going down of the sun
when the sky is all colours.

So I'm not so scared of the approaching dark.
It helps to know he's only a few feet away
and I don't have to wake Frederick.

I did die on the barbed wire
but that's behind me now.
Noel tells me I can choose not to remember.

At Home:

Francis Lloyd, Governor of London attends the Poplar Funerals—20th June 1917

Their coffins are so small.
Sixteen child-sized boxes
in the chancel
right next to me.

The church is crowded with mourners,
and their mothers and fathers.
I find the whole thing exceedingly affecting.

I have always had regrets
about not having a child of my own.
For once I am grateful to God in his wisdom.

Francis Lloyd's Administrative Duties—
July 1918

Rationing is extended to the whole country
including lard and sugar
but, for now, vegetables remain available.
We need to find more space to grow them in London.

I'm told Ina is waiting to see me.
I'm very fond of my niece.
Always a pleasure to have her company,
a respite from my administrative duties.

Her son Ian was posted missing last summer.
To my utter dismay Ina begs me
to tell her if there is even the smallest chance
that Ian might still be alive.

'Perhaps he has been taken prisoner?'
I have to be gentle as I remove her hopes.
There is no likelihood he is a prisoner of war.
No report in that regard has ever been received.

I've made two official visits to the Western front.
No buildings, trees cut down by the shelling.
No houses. No villages. Such desolation.

After she has gone I move back
to the wide expanse of my desk
and the welcome task
of making the flower beds
around the Victoria memorial
into vegetable gardens.

Edward Thomas at Gidea Park

You are amongst the legions,
men in khaki, waiting on the platform.
They are all young and you are pleased
to be caught up in their urgency.

On the same platform, there's a younger officer
named Owen, with a different company.
You'll never meet. Except, perhaps, on this occasion—
 getting your men onto the train.

You brush past, apologise for getting in his way,
then climb into the crowded carriage.
Something snags at your attention
like goose-grass caught on your sleeve.

You glance back, notice Owen's raised hand
his fingers are stained with ink
but the guard blows his whistle
and your train pulls away.

Gone to War

For Hedd Wyn

The military police seized you from hay-making,
for the crime of outstaying your leave to help with the harvest.
Your last poem left on the kitchen table.

Your hands which held a rifle wielded a pen
and that poem still in your head,
in the worst summer for rain anyone could remember.

Your poem got past the English Army censor.
Before the stretcher bearers found you, you'd laid wounded
in the midst of boys' screams dying in the wind
and Welsh blood thick as rain.

Your poems rise like ghosts of men.

The man who needed a tin nose

For Francis Derwent Wood

A great lump of my jaw is missing and half my nose.
Mercifully I was knocked out by the blast that did the damage.
The stretcher bearers had carried me to the dressing station
before I woke up.
It feels like a lifetime ago but was less than a year.
The surgeon has done his best to patch me back together
and now I've been sent to the shop for tin noses.

The Professor explains he will make me a mask.
He means well and told me before we started
he did not mind if I cried out
when he pressed clay into my face,
where my wounds have only just healed.

The word he used was 'whimper'.
He said, 'This may make you whimper
but that is allowed. I will not mind.'
I was determined not to give him the satisfaction.
He began on the complete side of my jaw
with handfuls of wet stuff.
When he got to the other part it hurt like hell.

What I did not realise was how he would carry on
until he covered my whole face, until I was shut in.
He got rather more than the whimper he expected.
I felt him pat my hand and he talked and talked
about how the mask would look, with suitable flesh tones,
as I fought to control myself and to stop sobbing.

The Professor of Sculpture

A few years ago these men might have been my students,
so young but the war has ripped pieces out of them.
Their appearance is beyond the skill of the surgeons to mend.
My task is seemingly simple, to devise new faces.
There are so many and each must have his own.
The world does not want reminders and these men
are a source of melancholy to themselves and their families.
My masks of copper as thin as a visiting card
can return them to themselves.
I work until exhaustion forces me asleep, still clothed
and wake to find I have drooled, an old man
attempting the impossible but the work must go on.

In the Royal Pavilion Hospital—
September 1915

Here I am being cared for by an orderly.
He has been taught a few phrases of Punjabi
and can ask if I am in pain, or hungry or thirsty.
Although I could understand if he spoke in English
I like the sound of the words made strange
by his odd way of saying them.
His skin is pale like milk.

I asked if he could write a letter
to my mother and sisters,
but when he brought pen and paper
the thoughts turned to stones in my mouth.
'He is gentle like a girl
and white like a lily flower.'
I could not tell this to my mother.
He fetched a cloth and water
and washed the distress from my face.
'Do not be upset. I can do it later.'

I have a wound in my shoulder
and he changes the dressings.
Another soldier, a rough old fellow,
roars abuse at my orderly.
It does hurt when he cleans our wounds
but I stand up to the pain
by watching his quiet concentration,
his fingernails like pink shells.

If I were like that other fellow
I would not shout when the orderly
took hold of me to direct the piss
into the bed pan.
Instead I would be grateful.

Who are you looking for?

The wooden roll of honour is shut away
behind a locked door,
in the hush of St Pancras church.

Anne, the vicar, asks
'Are you looking for relatives?
The names of all the 19th London regiment
are on the stained glass panels upstairs.
It is not normally open to visitors,
the gallery has a low slung parapet
and people might fall.'

Allenby led them into Jerusalem in 1917,
she tells us, he made a speech
ahead of its time about respect for different cultures.

Anne hopes to hold a service to remember them in 2017
but it's difficult with such a small congregation.

Two names follow me round for the rest of the day.
like children hoping for a picnic.
Sergeant Major J Baird who died two months after the armistice.
Private R Phillips—30th April 1918.

The Cooks' Story

19th London Regiment

We're foraging for edible greens
to supplement our supplies.
All armies march on their stomachs
and ours is no exception,
ain't finding much amongst the sand and rocks.

A group of men approaches holding small white flags on sticks.
Their leader, dressed all in black, flings himself on his knees.
'I beg you, do not storm my city.
I will give you the keys to Jerusalem.'

When we don't reply right away,
he throws himself face down.
My mate says 'Ere don't take on like that.'
We help him to his feet, tell him we're the cooks.
We take him and his flag bearers back to camp:
prisoners we hadn't meant to capture.

Turns out he is the Mayor,
out looking for General Allenby
to whom he could surrender.
My old lady will never believe me
but I do write and tell her.

For Charles Sargeant Jagger

You will not know what to make of me,
a woman who earns her own living.
You'll think of flappers, suffragettes,
unruly women but you'll be polite
and I determined to win you over.

I'll tell you people still love your statues.
Those men in bronze into whom
you breathed life,
they are part of the London landscape.
You'll pretend not to be pleased
but your eyes will give you away.

On learning I write poetry
you will ask if I like Kipling
and begin to recite as a kind of a test,
For what is sunk will hardly swim,
Not with this wind blowing, and this tide.
You say his son was amongst the missing.
I nod and we share a look of understanding.

I'll tell you about our national poets;
Carol, Sinead, Liz and Gillian.
You lean forward with great animation,
your younger daughter is named Gillian.

I know her work. She is a sculptor
and well known in the United States.
This time you won't disguise your pride.

I'll ask if we could walk to Hyde Park
so you can show me your memorial to the Royal Artillery.
You'll take my hand. Your grip surprisingly tender
with strength in your fingers
as you give mine a squeeze.
You'll explain we can go another time
when you're not feeling so tired.

Out in France and Flanders:

I walk in the battlefield cemeteries

'Move him into the sun' Wilfred Owen

The white headstones stand in ordered lines,
ranked across what was once a field.
Beneath the cropped green grass
are the memories and dreams of young men.

I walk from one headstone to the next,
reciting their names and the few words
their families were allowed.
'He did his best', 'How we loved him', 'Ever in our thoughts'.

I halt at the graves of those 'Known unto God'.
This task of remembering feels too much
for a mother of sons. I want to hug each boy
back to warmth, tell him he is not forgotten.

Hooge Crater Cemetery

Henry Evan's Viola

For Vanessa Gebbie

The Viola was so tiny among the short cemetery grass,
that only a person paying close attention
would notice the three rounded leaves
and its flower face opening to the sun.

In a few days the gardeners
will mow it down unnoticed.
It has seized its brief chance
to flower on the grass path.

You've come from Ringmer to find Henry Evans.
You scrape up the Viola with your finger nails,
its leaves, petals and twist
of tiny root to bring it home.

For Jeremy Banning, military historian

You have taught me how to read a cemetery like a story
and you unveil this landscape with a familiar intimacy.
Here is that wide field on which they died, sky-lined
with the dawn light behind them.
You bring back the dead so they walk with the living.

One of the Honeybills

It must have been taken in 1917.
The photographer has chosen a mottled background
reminiscent of rain and clouds.
Nothing detracts from your white sergeant's stripes.
Your eyes are like my grandfather's and you have his way
of gazing past the photographer as if
you can see into the future.

I see you, Percy Honeybill, but you could never imagine
someone would come a century on
to send your grandson into the attic
where he will find your diary and the jotted notes in the back.
Joined up Dec 1st 1916
Sent to Prees Dec 11th 1916
and the careful details during 1917
of promotion
to lance corporal
to lance sergeant.
There are no entries after September 1918.

So much is missing; the rest of your life
and even your body.
But in this photograph you do look happy.

For Victor at the Menin Gate

For the only beloved son of Robert Samuel and Mary Grace Davies, killed on 31st July 1917, aged 20, and all the Royal Welsh Fusiliers who died alongside him.

Where did you fall?
Somewhere out in the fields
the summer rain had turned to mud.

Where did you fall?
I cannot find the field corner
enriched with your Welsh blood.

Where did you fall?
There is only your name
among the thousands on a stone wall.

Wherever you fell,
I bring you a white rose, for peace,
Robert Victor Davies.

The Menin Gate

Acknowledgements and Notes

None of these poems would exist without the inspiration given to me by people both living and dead, and foremost are the men themselves who were caught up in the conflict and whose lives were consumed by it during and after the war.

The Litany—names taken from the Machynlleth War memorial with thanks to my uncle James for taking me to see it.

Skin I—Jane and Louise's Wilson's film and art installation Undead Sun at the Imperial War Museum, London, 2014.

Skin II—Paul Emmanuel's 'Lost Men' installation at Thiepval Memorial, 2014.

The Fusilier and the Sculptor—The Royal Fusilier (City of London Regiment) memorial at Holborn Bar, created by Mr Albert Toft (1862-1949). The man who modelled for the statue was believed to be called Sergeant Cox.

The Tommy statue at Flers—the memorial to the 41st Division in Flers, France which is a copy of the Royal Fusilier monument.

Glad of my men—the Oldham memorial to the men of the 1st, 10th and 24th Battalions, Manchester Regiment. The statue on top of the memorial is identical in appearance to the Royal Fusilier and the Tommy at Flers.

What Louis Doffman knows—For Louis Doffman, who served as Lewis Mountford in the 2nd Battalion, Worcestershire Regiment— may he forgive me for imagining his life.

Pigeon Ravine—for all 228 men of 2nd Battalion, Worcestershire Regiment, killed in Pigeon Ravine on 29th September 1918.

Peter Barton's Lessons of History—inspired by a lecture by military historian Peter Barton on his work at Fromelles, *The Lost Legions of Fromelles,* Constable and Robinson, London (2014) and at La Boisselle.

After being issued with SS456 Burial of Soldiers—for Private J McCauley, 2nd Border Regiment. SS456 were instructions issued by the Army regarding the identification of the dead.

Charles Sargeant Jagger—Inspired by the life and work of sculptor Charles Sargeant Jagger (1885—1934) including his service with 4th Battalion Worcestershire Regiment at Gallipoli, where he was wounded, and the 2nd Battalion Worcestershire Regiment on the Western Front, where he was awarded the Military Cross.

During the 1920s Jagger was responsible for many war memorials including:

- *Mr Jagger asks his tutor, Mrs Lilian Wade, to model for him*—Hoylake and West Kirby
- *Private Edwardes*—Hoylake and West Kirby
- *Designing the Great Western War Memorial—March 1921*—Paddington Station
- *Great Western War Memorial—December 1921*—Paddington Station
- *Planning the Royal Artillery Memorial*
- *After the unveiling of the Royal Artillery Memorial*

The Euston Road Mob—is based on the London and North Western Railway Company memorial at Euston Station. The four statues are the work of Reginald Wynn Owen, the railway architect and cast by Ambrose Neale of R L Boulton and sons. The National Archives at Kew hold the file RAIL 1057/2868 with information about the creation of the memorial and the unveiling ceremony, which took place on 21st October 1921. The poem appeared in *Envoi* June 2015. Albert, Frederick, Percy and George/ Noel are creations of my imagination but you can visit Euston Bus Station and see the statues.

At Home:

Francis Lloyd, Governor of London attends the Poplar Funerals—20th June 1917: Inspired by the memorial in Poplar for the eighteen children from Upper North Street School, killed in the first daylight bombing of London.

*Francis Lloyd's administrative duties—July 1918—*based on the life of Francis Lloyd, Governor of London with information taken from Richard Morris's book *The Man who ran London during the Great War,* Pen and Sword Books, 2010.

*Edward Thomas at Gidea Park—*inspired by a lecture given by Matthew Hollis on his book *Now all Roads lead to France,* Faber and Faber, London, 2011. An earlier version of this poem appeared in *Adlestrop Remembered: A Poetry Anthology from the Centenary Competition.*

*Gone to War—*the life of Ellis Humphrey Evans, known by his bardic name Hedd Wyn, and for all the men of the 15th Battalion Royal Welsh Fusiliers killed on Pilckem Ridge, Passchendaele on 31st July 1917 including my great uncle, Victor Davies.

The man who needed a tin nose and the *Professor of Sculpture—*the life of Francis Derwent Wood, sculptor (1871-1926).

Who are you looking for?—memorial to the 19th London (St.Pancras) Regiment, St Pancras Church Euston Road.

The Cook's story—memorial to the 19th London (St.Pancras) Regiment, St Pancras Church Euston Road.

Friends and Family:

Henry Evan's Viola—for Vanessa Gebbie who inspired and accompanied me every step of the way and whose book Memorandum is published by Cultured Lama Press in 2016.

For Jeremy Banning, military historian—friend, guide and teacher without whom this book would never have come into being.

One of the Honeybills—for Percy Honeybill (1887-1918) who was one of the Manchester Honeybills with thanks to his grandson Peter Jordan for allowing me use of his photograph and diary entries.

And finally for my great uncle, Robert Victor Davies (1897—1917) killed on the Pilkem Ridge on 31st July 1917 and for his mother, Mary Grace and sisters Bena and Edie who never had the opportunity to visit the Menin Gate where Victor is remembered:

For Victor at the Menin Gate